THE MARKET IS INCAPABLE OF CREATING ENOUGH JOBS:
Exposing the "Big Lie" by the Koch Brothers

By

Jim Green

DEDICATED TO:

Those who appreciate the premise presented here..........the
Dedication everyone who writes hopes to give regarding their
writings....but never do.......

ISBN-10: 1515166058

ISBN-13: 978-1515166054

PROLOGUE

THE market cannot provide everybody wanting a job, with a job—and knowing this is a big deal, a really a big deal—a really, really big deal—the data proving this is below, but the point, here, is that the propaganda, the "Big Lie" by the Koch Brothers [a metaphor, here, for the 1%--who have cornered America's wealth, and want even more]—i.e.., the big lie is that the market can provide everybody with a job, and this is, singularly, is our job creation methodology in America!

It is a lie....a joke!

And most Americans have been brainwashed into believing this lie! It is the reason why we stand on one foot and then the other [rather than revolting in the streets] waiting on market recovery to fix our unemployment crisis....

This is a really big deal because we have a serious unemployment problem in America—with oft dire social consequences...and as just one example...6 years in on our current recovery and we still have almost 9 million Americans still looking for work, who are unable to find work….

In short, we have a severe "social" problem in America—and we are getting a snow job that we have a solution! It is like waiting on Santa Clause….and the Koch Brothers want to keep it that way because the 1% still has one foot on the plantation, and want American employees without rights! Period!

And until we break this choke-hold we are not going to solve our unemployment crisis in America!

When Donald Trump, or any Republican for that matter, but, here, Trump talks about all the jobs he is going to bring back from China—or wherever—he is saying so because he "believes"—really believes----really, really believes…[as does every Republican]….that "the market can provide anybody wanting a job, with a job".

And it is through this prism that he is making this statement…

With Trump's ego, he is bloviating about a grandious claim that he will create thousands of businesses, if elected, which in turn will create these jobs…but what is missing in this grand scheme—if the market fails, the jobless are out of luck!

In short, Trump doesn't really have a job creation program he blathers on about...

And it is dishonest to sell a program as "fact", that is based on "belief"....i.e., a Santa Claus job creation program—based on wishful thinking—rather than fact! Indeed, the entire Republican job creation program will collapse into a pile of dirt...if we remove this fraud from their message....

I grew up in El Dorado, Kansas....down the road some 30 miles from Wichita, Kansas....and I heard of the Koch Brothers, before they were the Koch Brothers.....

And at the time Wichita was a hotbed for radical ideas [indeed, it appears the whole state of Kansas has gone nuts, now], i.e., the John Birch Society, etc.,—forerunners to the current term used to define this mind-set: "neo-liberalism" which seems best defined as Laissez-Faire on steroids....in short, *Greed* for the sake of *Greed*.....I got mine and screw you [the *Sole* Republican agenda, today]....

Specifically, since WW II, the Koch brothers [both literally, and a metaphor, throughout, for the plutocracy/oligarchy—which has a choke hold on America, today] have spent tens of millions buying governors and legislators, to cement "at will" employment in every state [only Montana limits to probationary employees]; and to destroy "collective bargaining", i.e., unions in America—

In sum, they have spent tens of millions of dollars to destroy "employee rights" in America!

To understand the importance of "collective bargaining" for employees, it is informative to take a page from history:

When Hitler became the dictator in Germany, one of his first laws was to make it illegal for more than three persons to gather on the street—and German citizens were subject to immediate arrest if they did.

The same principal is being used by preventing employees putting their heads together, as it were, to collectively bargain for employee rights—and recently one group of employees placed "job security" over a salary increase—with the irony being that the specific objective of "at will" employment—is to destroy "job security"!

In short, the deceptive propaganda to frighten Americans regarding "public-sector" jobs, has but a single parent: To exploit American labor—by some, to assuage deep-seated feelings of inferiority [they can only feel tall, by making others small, in their eyes]--—but most often for just pure GREED!

Where our policies makers go wrong by pandering to some in the oligarchy—and/or buying into this fraudulent propaganda.

Unemployment is a NO ONE WINS—the jobless lose, civility loses, and the market loses, to wit.

THE LAW OF DIMINISHED INCOME TO THE MARKET FROM UNEMPLOYMENT [hereafter D/UE LAW]

Short Definition.

> 3% is the zero-sum threshold above which unemployment starts substantially undermining the Market--and the loss in income to the Market is compounded exponentially with each percentage point of increase in unemployment, above 3%.

And where the Koch Brothers got it wrong is that in their tunnel-vision they fail to see that Public-Sector jobs strengthen our free-enterprise market economy—and given "automation", alone, public-sector jobs are a critical component to the viability of our 21st Century economy—

RATHER than weakening the market--as propagandist, with one foot on the plantation, fraudulently deceive the public.....public-sector jobs are *indispensable* to the *effective* functioning of a modern market economy!

In short, the Koch Brothers –the plutocracy/oligarchy is shooting itself in the foot by undermining public-sector jobs—the path we should be on, i.e., HR 1000, and Economic Inclusivism [neo-capitalism] solutions.

The mind-set that THE MARKET CAN PROVIDE ANYBODY WANTING A JOB, WITH A JOB ……is a passe thought…..never did work well…..but now, not at all….and, in fact, destructive to America going forward into the 21st Century….

A thumbnail of the points raised, here:

In the mid-1970's the world economy underwent a major paradigm shift—and while economists disagree over why—all agree with Dr. William F. Mitchell that "High and persistent unemployment has pervaded almost every OECD country since the mid-1970's" [with double digit unemployment common in the Eurozone to this day, and youth unemployment north of 25% in Greece and Spain]. As a result of high unemployment in the 1970's, America swung into action--and in 1978 Congress passed, and President Carter signed into law a "legal authorization" to henceforth limit America's unemployment rate to "3%" [15 USC § 3101—i.e., at not time should our unemployment exceed 3%, as provided by law]. With a ton of cash, however, the 1% has inexplicably prevented this law from ever being implemented. Full employment is a pro-market solution, and given "automation", alone, this law is *indispensable* to the *effective* functioning of our 21st Century economy. The purpose of this book is to urge the enforcement of this concept [currently HR 1000, in Committee].

A couple of related factors: In 1975 we spent $5 educating our youth, for every $1 we spent on prisons…..by the mid-1990's [with the American people having been terrorized by the Willie Horton ad—and on an hysterical prison building spree] our competing tax dollars tipped in favor of prisons—and at present we spend more on prisons, than on educating our youth.

The fact is: We have 5% of the world's population—and 25% [one in four] prison inmates, on Earth, in our prisons…and with disproportionate minority incarceration. It is impossible to correct our pernicious criminal justice system, however, until we correct the underlying systemic problems causing it—specifically, and almost singularly, our unwillingness to create an unemployment program in America.

At present we have NO job creation program in America, as we languish under the archaic belief that "the market can provide anybody wanting a job, with a job". In time, work will be a legal right in America—but at present, that is not even on the horizon and conservatives confuse a legal right to work—with the right to *look* for work—as different as night to day....

In short, critical in reforming our criminal justice system—is creating a job creation program in America.

A few closing comments in the Prologue—As Oscar Wilde averred "The only truly worthless opinion is an unbiased one"—so bias, agreed—but always in the interest in getting at the larger goal—the truth....

Incidentally, I published my first book on my 78th birthday—and not that I write that fast, or well—the materials were all there for the better part of the past 30 years, give or take, gathering dust— it was just a matter of pulling them together in some order—also, don't believe any book should be over 60 pages, plus/minus— i.e., can be read in the crapper--two hours, max--lol—but it seems best summed up by a very astute observer [wish I could recall their name to give credit]: Persons who write do so because they have no choice [it is a compulsion, an addiction..]—they become an "author", however, when people start reading what they have written....

Finally, a note to the reader—the papers and letters are not in sequence, and apologize for redundancy [please look for the nuggets…Thx--lol]—also, if you are a "typo-wonk"—are more concerned with sentence structure, etc., than content—you probably won't like my writing—and you will find a wayward capital letter, here and there, and appearing out of place and used for emphasis—or a missing page…Hey, I'm and Indie….I chalk most up to editorial license and tongue-in-cheek, self-effacing humor—so apologies, here—[I seriously support: Take what you do seriously, but never yourself….]….

Just look for content, please….THX

CHAPTER ONE

The day following President Obama's historic trip to the El Reno Federal Prison, in Oklahoma—7/16/15

President Obama:

It is impossible to reform our broken criminal justice system—absent our creating a viable job creation program in America.

And while it is generally believed that we do have a job creation program, in fact, we do not!

We have the BELIEF that "the market can provide anybody wanting a job, with a job"—but the data shows that only ONCE since WW II has this belief resulted in an unemployment rate below 3%--in 1953—leaving millions jobless in its wake-- and has resulted in:

60% minority unemployment in our inner-cities, with drug economies, and an epidemic of homicides [i.e., not fixing unemployment has turned our inner-cities into war zones, and created a breeding ground for our inexplicable incarceration rate].

Further this "belief" has been a stumbling block in finding a solution for our pervasive unemployment--In short, we have not been looking for a solution—because our policy makers believe we have one—and apparently few have looked at the data....

Also, ignored in the discussion is that unemployment is a "social" problem, with adverse, and oft severe social consequences—both for the individual, as well as the larger society [i.e., it is the responsibility of the larger society to solve]—

With tentacles integral to all of the social problems facing Americans, today—for instance, ending unemployment is integral to Criminal Justice Reform, and the repair of our crumbling infrastructure....

Further, in 1975 we spent $5 educating our youth, for every $1 we spent on prisons.....by the mid-1990's [with the American people having been terrorized by the Willie Horton ad—and on an hysterical prison building spree] our competing tax dollars tipped in favor of prisons—and at present we spend more on prisons, than on educating our youth.

The irony in all of this is that we have the "legal authorization", on the books to reduce our unemployment rate to 3%, tomorrow [15 USC § 3101—and deficit-neutral HR 1000, currently in

Committee]—and also ignored in this context, is that President Obama had a weapon in addressing our economic meltdown in 2008, not available to FDR—and that is the $800 billion in Social Security Insurance claims percolating up through our economy—and in the absence of which--We would be buried in another Great Depression!

Turning the page—and given "automation", alone, is critical going forward in the 21st Century—and is a "win-win"—the American people win, and the market wins....

Ref: FULL EMPLOYMENT IS A PRO-MARKET CONCEPT, Amazon

Jim Green, Democrat opponent to Lamar Smith, 2000

CHAPTER TWO

President Obama/Council of Economic Advisers:

Our network of market-driven economies [the OECD, including the U.S]—currently have a pernicious job creation modality—with resulting high and pervasive unemployment since the mid-1970's—and on a collision course with the future—i.e., given "automation", alone, fewer and fewer jobs are being created with each passing year, as we advance into the 21st Century....

This job creation modality is based on the erroneous propaganda/belief that "the market can provide anybody wanting a job, with a job"—and yet, only ONCE since WW II has this modality resulted in an unemployment rate below 3%--in 1953—leaving millions jobless in its wake, and has resulted in our inner-cities turning into war zones--with 60% minority unemployment, drug economies, and an epidemic of homicides.

The irony in this disaster, however, is that the U.S. correctly anticipated this result in 1978—and provided the American people with a solution, i.e., the "legal authorization" [15 USC § 3101] to limit our unemployment henceforth to "3%", and as we advance into the 21st Century—

With a ton of cash poured into our political system, and a mind-set with both feet planted on the plantation—---special interests sabotaged this law to prevent its implementation—to the detriment of Americans, and America [ISIS is the least of our worries in America, when we have the Republican party]!

Unemployment is a "social" problem, with adverse social consequences….it is solely the province of the larger society to solve—and leaving the solution to anything as erratic as the market—as we do now—is patently absurd!

The bottom line is that unemployment is a NO ONE WINS….the jobless lose, civility loses, and the market loses, to wit:

THE LAW OF DIMINISHED INCOME TO THE MARKET FROM UNEMPLOYMENT [hereafter D/UE LAW]

3% is the zero-sum threshold above which unemployment triggers inflation by diminishing labor training and skills, under-utilizing capital resources, reducing the rate of productivity advance, increasing unit labor costs, reducing the general supply of goods and services--and the loss in income to the Market is compounded exponentially with each percentage point of increase in unemployment, above 3%.

Ref: HR 1000 [in Committee], and FULL EMPLOYMENT IS A PRO-MARKET SOLUTION, Amazon

Jim Green, Democrat opponent to Lamar Smith, 2000

Thank You!

Thank you for contacting the White House

CHAPTER THREE

POSTED ON FACEBOOK:

An "Aha moment"--Texas is either under attack by the U.S. Army....Or....the Republican party is under attack by crazy people....Aha...now we know why the House is filled with lunatics who think obstructing President Obama [because he is black] is "a program", and why Ted Cruz was elected, and why Trump is making outlandish xenophobic statements to pander to our "crazy people"—to get their vote....See: IT IS IMPOSSIBLE TO BE A CHRISTIAN, AND VOTE REPUBLICAN, Amazon/Kindle

The factions Trump [actually, all of the Republican candidates] is seeking to get in his corner are our racists, literal thinkers [with "thinkers" exceedingly generous], and our hate mongers [they hate everybody including themselves]—and absent these factions his poll numbers would vanish. See: FULL EMPLOYMENT IS A PRO-MARKET CONCEPT, Amazon/Kindle

CHAPTER FOUR

President Obama/Council of Economic Advisers:

Public-Sector jobs strengthen our free-enterprise market economy—i.e., they are a critical component to the viability of our 21st Century economy--rather than weakening the market-- as propagandist, with one foot on the plantation, fraudulently deceive the public into believing for the purposes of exploiting American employees......

Indeed, since WW II, the Koch brothers [both literally, and a metaphor, here, for the 1%] have spent tens of millions buying governors and legislators, to cement "at will" employment in every state [and currently only Montana limits to probationary employees]; and to destroy "collective bargaining", i.e., unions in America—

In sum, they have spent tens of millions of dollars to destroy "employee rights" in America!

To understand the importance of "collective bargaining" for employees, it is informative to take a page from history:

When Hitler became the dictator in Germany, one of his first laws was to make it illegal for more than three persons to gather on the street—and German citizens were subject to immediate arrest if they did.

The same principal is being used by preventing employees putting their heads together, as it were, to bargain for employee rights—and recently one group of employees placed "job security" over a salary increase—with the irony being that the specific objective of "at will" employment—is to destroy "job security"!

In short, the deceptive propaganda to frighten Americans regarding "public-sector" jobs, has but a single parent. To exploit American labor—by some, to assuage deep-seated feelings of inferiority [they can only feel tall, by making others small, in their eyes]--—but most often for just pure GREED!

Where our policies makers go wrong by pandering to some in the oligarchy—and/or buying into this fraudulent propaganda.

Unemployment is a NO ONE WINS—the jobless lose, civility loses, and the market loses, to wit.

THE LAW OF DIMINISHED INCOME TO THE MARKET FROM UNEMPLOYMENT [hereafter D/UE LAW]

Short Definition:

3% is the zero-sum threshold above which unemployment
starts substantially undermining the Market--and the loss
in income to the Market is compounded exponentially with
each percentage point of increase in unemployment, above
3%.

Ref: IT IS IMPOSSIBLE TO BE A CHRISTIAN, AND VOTE
REPUBLICAN, Amazon

Jim Green, Democrat opponent to Lamar Smith, 2000

CHAPTER FIVE

President Obama/Council of Economic Advisers:

THE JULY 2015 JOBS REPORT

If one believes that "the market can provide anybody wanting a job, with a job"—then the case can be made to "jump start" the market, and this will, in turn, fix unemployment—and this was the mind-set when HR 2847 [The Hire Act] became law.

At the time, however, we had 10.2% unemployment [hereafter UE] and the adverse consequences of UE has been left to wait as the economy inched towards recovery.

And it has taken us 6 years to shave 4.9 points off of our UE rate, and we are still left with 8.3 million Americans looking for work, who are unable to find work.

This having been said, however, it is little wonder why we Democrats celebrate that we are moving in a positive direction—given the vitriolic climate in Washington—and it would be a fool's errand to expect the current crop of Republicans to actually look for a solution to our unemployment crisis—but that is all the more reason to chart a different path.

The operative phrase here is "the adverse consequences of unemployment" and left out of the discussion is that UE is a "social" problem, with adverse social consequences—i.e., we, the larger society have the absolute responsibility to address....

And our indifference has become a breeding ground for ISIS sympathizers in America [and throughout the OECD]—even disregarding that this mind-set has resulted in 60% minority UE in our inner-cities, with a drug culture, and an epidemic of homicides.

The job creation mind-set that "the market can provide anybody wanting a job, with a job" [which the Republicans fraudulently report as "fact"]—has never been true, and only ONCE since WW II has it resulted in a UE rate below 3%--in 1953—leaving millions jobless in its wake, and created the inner-cities, above.

86% of Americans believe that "anybody wanting to work, should be able to find a job"—i.e., there is solid political support for the "legal authorization" in Public Law 15 USC § 3101 to limit our unemployment to "3%" [essentially full employment], and reiterated in HR 1000, currently in Committee.

In short, at no time should our UE rate in America exceed 3%, as provided by law.

Ref: WHY DO WE AMERICANS ACCEPT BEING AN "INDEX" IN OUR ECONOMIC SYSTEM, Amazon

Jim Green, Democrat opponent to Lamar Smith, Congress, 2000

CHAPTER SIX

EDITOR, NY TIMES

Some in the media keep referring to U.S. Senator Bernie Sanders as a "socialist", but with the election well over a year away, and his drawing crowds of 10,000, we need to ask:

We either have an awful lot of socialists in America—or we need to re-think the words being thrown around to sabotage our finding solutions to the myriad of problems, Republicans and Democrats alike, face in America?

For instance, it is mind-shattering that the all together decent word "liberal" is constantly trashed by Limbaugh, and his ilk—it is obvious Limbaugh doesn't have a clue what the word means!

First, the most prized education one can have is a "liberal education"—it means one is open-minded, receptive to new ideas—and the last thing we want to be identified as is the opposite of liberal—i.e., "illiberal", which Webster's defines as: "small-minded, petty, bigoted, stingy".

Another couple of other words that have become toxic, and are used to sabotage discussion, are the words "communism" and "socialism".

And ever since McCarthy crawled out of the swamps in the 1950's, and frightened Americas into believing we have a "commie behind every tree"—America has been wounded ever since—with the word "commie" thrown around constantly by those on the right to sabotage discussion.

But what do the words "communism" and " socialism" mean?

Communism: The government owns and runs our commerce, and the abolition of private property.

I do not know of even one person who thinks this is a good idea, and frankly I do not know of even one Democrat who is not a capitalist—so other than just plain ignorance or stupidity, it is meaningless to call a Democrat a "commie".

Further, fascism and communism are on the two political extremes—and it requires a dictator to hold the government in place—and Democrats are vehemently opposed to our ever having a dictator in America.

Socialism: Marx saw socialism as the transitional stage where capitalism moved to communism—but includes government running commerce—which is a really bad idea, with one major exception, and this is where Bernie Sanders and millions of other Americans comes in—he supports "single-payer" healthcare.

The message, here, is be chary of labels from every Republican—Al Franken had it right "Rush Limbaugh is a big, fat, idiot"!

Jim Green, Democrat candidate for Congress, 2000

CHAPTER SEVEN

Council of Economic Advisers:

The ancient English proverb "There's many a slip twixt the cup and the lip" could not be more true as regards our addressing unemployment in America, today....

Unemployment [hereafter UE] is a "social" problem with not infrequent dire social consequences—

And yet, our job creation in America, is based on the erroneous premise: "an erratic market can provide anybody wanting a job, with a job" [only ONCE since WW II has this resulted in a UE rate below 3%--in 1953—leaving millions jobless in its wake—and by omission, has turned our inner-cities into war zones]....

In short, under this mind-set, our job creation policies have been driven by the premise "Fix the market, and this will fix UE" [HR 2847]—

Rather than the exact opposite path--which we should have been on [HR 1000]: "Fix UE, and this will fix the market" [which would have prevented a slow drip in our UE recovery, with prolonged dire social consequences—it has taken us 6 years to shave an anemic 4.9% from our UE rate]…and under our current methodology--if the market fails, the jobless are out of luck!

Further, ignored in this dynamic: As a "social" problem—we as the larger society have the absolute responsibility to step up to the plate on behalf of our fellow citizens—the same as we did with the GI Bill, and Social Security Insurance.

In sum, our methodology for solving the most pernicious social problem facing America today--is wholly inadequate to the task—with the result our consummate proof…..a methodology, incidentally, from an oligarchy which still has one foot on the plantation, and is saddled with 18th Century solutions, in a 21st Century world…..

And the compelling question, today: If South Carolina can change—surely, inside the Beltway can turn the page?

Unemployment is a No One Wins: The jobless lose, civility loses, and the market loses, to wit:

THE LAW OF DIMINISHING INCOME TO THE MARKET FROM UNEMPLOYMENT [hereafter D/UE LAW]

Short Definition:

3% is the zero-sum threshold above which unemployment starts substantially undermining the Market--and the loss in income to the Market is compounded exponentially with each percentage point of increase in unemployment, above 3%.

Ref: ECONOMIC INCLUSIVISM: Inclusive Pro-Market Solutions to our Social Problems, Amazon

Jim Green, Democrat opponent to Lamar Smith, 2000

CHAPTER EIGHT

Letter to Senator Sanders:

Senator Sanders: 86% of Americans believe that "anybody wanting to work, should be able to find a job"—and yet, Washington doesn't have a clue how to solve this, the most pernicious problem facing America, today: UNEMPLOYMENT! And, someone must tell the American people that the market CANNOT provide everyone wanting a job, with a job—it is the "Big Lie" that drives our job creation in America, today, with a resulting 60% minority unemployment [hereafter UE] in our inner-cities—drug economies, and an epidemic of homicides. The point is that we [as well as all of the OECD] have severe UE problems—and we are being lied to that the market can solve this problem—In fact, only ONCE since WW II has this job creation method resulted in an UE rate below 3%--in 1953—leaving millions jobless in its wake, and created the inner-cities, above. And given "automation", alone, this problem will get exponentially worse as we advance into the 21st Century. In Sum, HR 1000 [in Committee] is critical in solving our unemployment crisis going forward, and is a Pro-Market solution.

Ref: FULL EMPLOYMENT IS A PRO-MARKET SOLUTION, Amazon/Kindle

Jim Green, Democrat opponent to Lamar Smith, 2000

Thank You

Thank you for contacting me.

CHAPTER NINE

WHAT WE NEED TO DO GOING FORWARD IN THE 21ST CENTURY:

Inexplicably "public employment" is seen the same as WPA—where millions are employed directly by the federal government—when that model is not only outmoded—it is insufficient to address our problems in the 21st century.

What we need today is an expanding and contracting public workforce—that expands during downturns in the market, and contracts as employees return to the private sector [Google: The Buffer Stock Employment Model]—triggered anytime our unemployment exceeds "3%" [as "authorized" under Humphrey-Hawkins]--and least understood: This is an INDISPENSABLE component in the effective functioning of our 21st Century Market.

The market thrives when we have a robust, employed, consuming workforce—our manufacturers are sitting on $2 trillion in cash because they do not have consumers for their products—i.e., absent consumers, they lay off employees—[and the Republican solution, Reaganomics, has acted as an accelerate to this downward spiral—and which Romney promises to return us to if he is elected]!

In short, the above model is a "win-win" solution—the American people win, and capitalism wins!

To achieve this, what is being urged is "The Neighbor-To-Neighbor Job Creation Act": A federally mandated, mutual insurance—owned by our employed [from janitor to CEO] to create a fund to hire/train our unemployed.

To be viable, however, our job creation solution _MUST_ contain:

1] Be based on the premise that we have far more work that needs to be done in America, than we have persons to fill these jobs.

2] It MUST have renewable funding.

3] It will not add a dime to our deficit.

To expand briefly, it is currently believed, erroneously, that we need "make work" jobs so that everyone who wants to work will have a job—but this is absurd—and an insult to "Yankee Ingenuity".

We do not have an unemployment crisis from a shortage of jobs, or money—but rather from a shortage of imagination.

Regarding "renewable funding" ALL of our job creation solutions, to date, have been based on the mind-set: "jump start" the market, and the market will in turn create all the jobs we need—and even setting aside that this is untrue, our current job creation is moving at a snail's pace—long past the unemployment benefits drying up—with the CBO projecting that even with the JOBS Act, signed into law on April 6, 2012--it will be 2017 before we return to a barely acceptable 5.5% unemployment rate!

Further, by its nature when we "jump start" --the employment ends when the funding runs out as we learned from the Stimulus—whereas any real fix to our unemployment crisis _demands_ renewable funding....

And whether the electorate will accept an unemployment rate hovering around 8% on election day—is the $64,000 question....

Regarding not adding a dime to our deficit—under The Neighbor-To-Neighbor Job Creation Act [NTN], the _funding_ to reduce our unemployment to 3% comes from an insurance owned by our employed, rather than added to our deficit—

If one is employed in America, participation in this insurance plan is mandatory—similar in concept to our auto insurance or Social Security Insurance [and without question the most successful social program in American history].

Jobs beget jobs--And with a modest policy cost of 4% of salary we can create more "private-sector" jobs in 6 months, that HR 2847, and the JOBS Act, in 6 years—and unlike these laws—NTN will not add a dime to our deficit!

Finally, this is in total concert with the will of the American people, i.e., that "anybody willing to work should be able to find a job"—and the American people have told our politicians time and again of their willingness to chip in to help their neighbor get a job [and as an _insurance_, as above, it also protects their continued employment]—it is just that Washington is deaf as an adder!

CHAPTER TEN

THE HISTORY OF HOW WE GOT WHERE WE ARE:

In the mid-1970's, the colliding forces of automation, technology, globalization, etc., reached a critical mass, resulting in ubiquitous unemployment in all of the OECD countries, and has left their leaders conflicted, ever since, regarding the displaced employee— Eurozone unemployment is still in double digits, with Spain at 22.9%, and with high youth unemployment a major factor in Arab Spring.

In the U.S., we took a pro-active role in addressing, and as a direct response to this economic shift—and in 1978 President Carter signed into law 15 USC § 3101--which "authorizes" the creation of a "reservoir of public employment" at any time our unemployment in America exceeds "3%".

The following year, in 1979, however, and in a panic over Humphrey-Hawkins—our ultra-conservative foundations, and desperate to preserve the "market only" job creation concept, embraced a flawed paper by an obscure MIT student, David L. Birch "The Job Generation Process"; and [with lots of cash] gave his paper biblical importance, and every president since has cited his finding as gospel.

Birch's paper concluded that "small businesses" were the greatest generator of new jobs—problem is, for the purposes of policy-making—it is BS. In a study at Harvard University in 2010, "The Myth of Small Business Job Creation" The research shows "no systematic relationship between firm size and growth." And that small businesses can actually detract from job growth—nevertheless, it is still the Republican One and Only job creation solution!

And in spite of this Washington struggles, still, to make this antiquated and unworkable notion, work--that it is only the market that can create jobs—the world has changed, our solutions haven't, and the result has been a disaster, politically as well as otherwise!

It would be impossible to still have 8.3% unemployment if we were on the right path [the result is the proof]—and among other problems with this concept--if the market fails, the unemployed are out of luck [It is the reason Romeny's job creation solution is a farce!].

Further, unemployment is a "social" problem we are seeking to address with a highly unstable, incompatible entity: The Market –

–That is, the last place we should look for a reliable solution to our unemployment crisis is The Market….

And, what apparently isn't clear going forward in the 21st Century, is that an expanding and contracting public workforce is an INDISPENSABLE component to the correct functioning of a modern market economy—i.e., The Humphrey-Hawkins Full Employment Act was dead-on correct in 1978—and provided a "win-win" solution for America--

The market thrives when we have a robust, employed, consuming workforce, and it is essential to consumer confidence—and overlooked is that HR 1000 [currently in Committee], and the proposed "Neighbor-To-Neighbor Job Creation Act" [1] -- hereafter NTN—See also: www.Inclusivism.org [both authorized under Humphrey-Hawkins], are deficit-neutral -Pro-Market "win-win" solutions: The American people win, and capitalism wins—

[1] PROPOSED LEGISLATION:

THE NEIGHBOR-TO-NEIGHBOR JOB CREATION ACT

A Pro-Market, deficit-neutral, federally mandated, Social Insurance, owned by our employed, to provide a fund to hire/train our unemployed.

SECTION 1. SHORT TITLE.

This Act shall be cited as The Neighbor-To-Neighbor Job Creation Act [To establish employment/training opportunities for the unemployed in compliance with the "Legal Authorization" in Public Law 15 USC § 3101, for the creation of a "reservoir of public employees", anytime our unemployment rate exceeds "3%", with an emphasis on training for market needs, including a training stipend, where there is a shortage of trained workers--hereafter NTN].

SEC. 2. DEFINITIONS.

In this Act the following definitions apply:
    (1) SECRETARY- The term `Secretary' means the Secretary of Labor.
    (2) STATE- The term `State' has the meaning given such term in section 102(2) of the Housing and Community Development Act (42 U.S.C. 5302(2)).
    (3) TRUST FUND- The term `Trust Fund' refers to the Department of Labor Full Employment Trust Fund.
    (4) UNIT OF GENERAL LOCAL GOVERNMENT- The term `unit of general local government' has the meaning given such term in section 102(1) of the Housing and Community Development Act (42 U.S.C. 5302(1)).
    (5) URBAN COUNTY- The term `urban county' has the meaning given such term in section 102(6) of the Housing and Community Development Act (42 U.S.C. 5302(6)).
    (6) WEB SITE- The Secretary shall establish an Internet Web site to serve as an information clearinghouse for job training and employment opportunities funded by the Trust Fund.

SEC. 3. EMPLOYMENT OPPORTUNITY GRANTS TO STATES, LOCAL GOVERNMENT.

(a) Use of Funds-A recipient of a grant under this section shall use the grant primarily for infrastructure repair, including, but not limited to:

> (A) The painting and repair of schools, community centers, and libraries.
> (B) The restoration and revitalization of abandoned and vacant properties to alleviate blight in distressed and foreclosure-affected areas of a unit of general local government.
> (C) The augmentation of staffing in Head Start, child care, and other early childhood education programs to promote school readiness and early literacy.
> (D) The renovation and enhancement of maintenance of parks, playgrounds, and other public spaces.

Respectfully Submitted,

Jim Green, Democrat candidate for Congress, Dist 21, TX, 2000

CHAPTER ELEVEN

President Obama/Council of Economic Advisers:

THE HISTORY OF HUMPHREY-HAWKINS

The historic March On Washington, and Dr. King's "I had a dream" speech, in 1963, was a march for JOBS.

At that time, and to this day, our job creation in America has been based on the premise that "the market can provide anybody wanting a job, with a job—

And yet, only ONCE since WW II has this method of job creation resulted in an unemployment rate below 3%--in 1953—leaving millions jobless in its wake.

Following Dr. Kings death in 1968, civil rights leaders, including Jesse Jackson, annually marched on Dr. King's birthday for legislation that would address our pervasive unemployment in America.

Their demand was not without legal foundation. In 1946, President Truman signed into law the [FULL] EMPLOYMENT ACT

OF 1946, to provide employment for our troops returning from WW II.

The 1%, however, balked at American employees having rights—particularly a right to employment [the model which exists to this day]—and the law was never implemented.

Ironically, Australia enacted a law similar to President Truman's Employment Act—and for the same reason—and for the next 30 years [and until the ill-winds of neo-liberalism in the mid-1970's] Australia's employment model was based on the premise that "anybody wanting to work should be able to find a job"—with 2% or less unemployment common. Australians still refer to this as their "Golden Age".

As a result of the demand by civil rights leaders for legislation, however, in 1978 President Carter signed into law—what is commonly known as the Humphrey-Hawkins Full Employment Act [15 USC § 3101].

The law provides the "legal authorization" for the creation of a "reservoir of public employees" anytime our unemployment in America exceeds "3%". That is, and to this day—at no time should our unemployment rate in America exceed 3%.

The money in politics, however, has prevented this law from being implemented!

Notwithstanding, a lone Congressman, Conyers [and a growing number of co-sponsors] has diligently worked to implement Humphrey-Hawkins [currently, deficit-neutral HR 1000, in Committee].

And, singularly, unemployment is the most pernicious problem facing America, today....

Ref: FULL EMPLOYMENT IS A PRO-MARKET CONCEPT, Amazon

Jim Green, Democrat opponent to Lamar Smith, 2000

Thank You!

Thank you for contacting the White House.

CHAPTER TWELVE

President Obama/Council of Economic Advisers:

THE WAR AGAINST AMERICAN EMPLOYEES HAVING RIGHTS

The word "war" may sound a bit strong, but rest assured—IT IS A WAR, a war the American people and our economy are losing, and millions of Americans have been injured as a result!

Since WW II we have passed two major pieces of legislation to address insidious unemployment [hereafter UE] in America, and in both cases the money in politics has prevented these laws from being implemented.

As a result, our inner-cities have 60% minority UE, with drug cultures, and an epidemic of homicides.

The laws in question are the [FULL] EMPLOYMENT ACT OF 1946, signed into law by President Truman, and in 1978, the HUMPHREY–HAWKINS FULL EMPLOYMENT ACT [15 USC § 3101], signed into law by President Carter.

86% of Americans believe that "anybody wanting to work should be able to find a job", and the latter provides Americans with the "legal authorization" to create a "reservoir of public employees" anytime our UE rate rises above "3%". That is, at no time, and until this day, should our UE rate in America exceed 3%.

Since WW II, however, tens of millions have been spent buying governors and legislators to cement "at will" employment in every state [only Montana limits to probationary employees]; and to destroy the union movement in America.

Running in concert to the abolition of employee rights in America, we have been sold Snake Oil, duped into believing that "the market can provide anybody wanting a job, with a job"—which would be ideal if true, but, in fact, it is pure BS!

And only ONCE since WW II has this resulted in a UE rate below 3%--in 1953—leaving millions jobless in its wake—and created the inner-cities, above.

What may turn the corner is the fact that UE is a "No One Wins"—the jobless lose, civility loses, and the market loses, to wit:

THE LAW OF DIMINISHED INCOME TO THE MARKET FROM UNEMPLOYMENT [hereafter D/UE LAW]

Short Definition:

3% is the zero-sum threshold above which unemployment starts substantially undermining the Market--and the loss in income to the Market is compounded exponentially with each percentage point of increase in unemployment, above 3%.

Turning the corner is a "win-win"—the American people win, and the market wins....

Ref: HR 1000 & FULL EMPLOYMENT IS A PRO-MARKET CONCEPT, Amazon

Jim Green, Democrat opponent to Lamar Smith, 2000

CHAPTER THIRTEEN

FAIL-SAFE ELECTRONIC VOTING

TO THE READER: Given you have gotten this far, and agree with the proposed changes—and particularly given the pernicious Citizens United—our democracy, and the above, or any, progress, will be in peril absent a "fail-safe" electronic voting system. The following is my proposed solution, and like every solution proposed, here, feed-back--your proposed improvement, etc. is welcomed.

THE FAIL-SAFE ELECTRONIC VOTING ACT

1) EVERY electronic voting machine (hereafter EVM), must be inexpensive, identical throughout the U.S. in a 1/150 ratio, and *must count and produce a hard-copy of the recorded votes.* In addition, an extra copy of their recorded votes would be produced (not necessarily a hard-copy), marked "Voter's Copy", and containing "NOTICE: Do Not Destroy Until Every Election On Your Ballot Is Certified". [If Wal-Mart handed us a piece of paper with the words "trust us" as a receipt for our purchases—we would be outraged—and yet, this is our current electronic voting nightmare—but in this case it is our democracy at risk]!

2) *After confirming that their votes are recorded correctly,* the voter would then insert the hard-copy ballot into a software-free (count only) optical scanner (hereafter OS), for a second count. The hard-copy ballot would be retained by election officials in the event a candidate asks for a recount (*not possible under the current system, and which undermines the legality of each such election).* The EVM and the OS must be manufactured by different companies (which is universally true today).

3) Election officials assigned to oversee the EVM, would be prevented by law from overseeing the OS, and vice-versa, and stiff criminal penalties would be imposed for violations.

4) Further, every EVM would be programmed with raw data re the total registration rolls, by party, and norms for their voting history, etc.,----as an "alert" to a possible irregularity, such as an "under-vote"—or "vote-flipping" etc., and *standards* established to suspend certification where there is an "improbable result", at least temporarily, of a particular election until the discrepancy is cleared up. (This is what computers do best, and it would be very easy to create such a program).

5) At the end of the election day, tallies would be taken from the EVM and the OS, for each candidate. *If the tallies didn't balance for any given election, or if there is an "alert", that election cannot be certified until the "error" is corrected.* If the candidates agree

(the victory is certain), minor discrepancies in the count could be disregarded. While probably rare, the Voter, or a random sample of Voters, would be required by law to return their Copy of the recorded votes to the election office to clear up any "error", or where an "alert" signals the need for same.

6) Further, every state provides for a recount when the total vote falls below a certain percent of difference between the candidates, impossible to conduct with the current EVM. And thus Congress must mandate the following regarding presidential candidates: A RUN-OFF election is mandated and triggered in those states where the percent of total vote is less than .5% of difference between the two candidates; said election to be held on the second Saturday following the election, on PAPER BALLOTS ONLY, and contain ONLY the names of the relevant candidates, for instance: "Barack Obama, Democrat" and "John McCain, Republican"— with oversight in counting by a representative(s) of each party— said procedure providing more than adequate time to meet the Electoral College mandate [Ideally, all of this could be eliminated if we did away with the Electoral College, but until then....]. NOTE: Had this been the law in 2000, Al Gore would be our president, and America would have been spared the economic, etc., disaster that followed!

7) Finally, absent the above safeguards, and until these safeguards are in place--Congress must mandate that PAPER BALLOTS,

ONLY, can be used in our presidential elections. This is not a "partisan" issue, it is a "pro-democracy" issue. Most importantly, this will return the responsibility for our elections, and our vote counting, back into the hands of the individual voter, where it belongs, and out of the hands of "corporate control"---_it is after all "our democracy", itself, that is at risk if we don't take these steps---and in that regard, is there any time or cost differential that is too great?_

Jim Green

CHAPTER FOURTEEN

I didn't write the following. It is a cut and paste from FACEBOOK, or some blog [would like to give credit if knew the author]--but it is so on target regarding how "fear" is driving Conservative policy in America today—i.e., is undermining America and our progress—and relegating America to a Third World country status, rather than a world leader—FDR had it on the nose in "All we have to fear, is fear itself"...at his inaugural in 1933....

"Conservatives are such cowards: they are afraid of gay people getting married or serving in the military; they are afraid of bringing terrorists to super max prisons in the US from which no one has ever escaped; they are afraid of the boy scouts letting gay kids in; they are afraid of everyone voting and are constantly suppressing the vote under some bogus voter fraud theory; they are afraid of letting students vote at their universities; they are afraid of women having the right to choose; they even are afraid of women getting contraception [the real issue actually is a women's agency and control over their bodies]; they are afraid of immigration reform leading to citizenship because they are afraid of-- name whatever reason; they are afraid of mandating gun purchasers to undergo background checks for crazy people and terrorists; they are afraid of people smoking pot; they are afraid of climate change being real and contradicting their beloved Bible;

they are afraid of legitimate campaign reform; they are afraid of Muslims; they are afraid of blacks; they are afraid of atheists; they are afraid of hippies; they are afraid of socialists; they are probably still afraid of monsters under their beds; they are just rank cowards and keep making things up to be afraid of."

CHAPTER FIFTEEN

[I couldn't resist including this…and yes I am the author…..]

A MESSAGE FROM GOD

MANY CENTURIES AGO, a man of the cloth, we don't know his name, and in a flash of insight (perhaps induced by peyote) told his flock that "sex is a sin". And lo and behold he learned that by taking a very natural and healthy part of our life and turning it into something that was "dirty and nasty", that he could imprison his flock, and fill his coffers, and hallelujah it was a great day for the Lord!

Quickly, his miracle spread to other churches in his village, and then to the next village, and then the next county, and then state, and soon it spread to all the churches in the ancient world, and all of their flocks cowed in fear and shame and became imprisoned, and their coffers over-floweth. Hallelujah, it was a great day for the Lord!

And to keep the myth alive they started inventing stories, half-baked stories, that made no sense to anyone who is rational, such as "Mary was a virgin"—well, she just had to be a virgin because she would never partake in anything that was dirty and nasty, like sex (if you're doing it right), and this was necessary to make "sex is a sin" make sense...so they invented a Mary that was "sinless"--you get the picture. And their coffers over-floweth. Hallelujah, it was a great day for the Lord!

No one seemed to be bothered that when we play tricks on the human mind by taking something that is very natural and healthy, such as sex, and make it dirty and nasty that all kinds of bad things happen to the human mind:

Such as most pedophiles, and most serial killers, and voting Republican, and unwarranted suicides, and most mental illness, and unwanted pregnancies. (Teens not wanting to have sex is the perversion, not the other way around, and by replacing sex education and condoms, with unrealistic "abstinence", and by using blather about "low self-esteem" to shame them into not "sinning"—We have a teen pregnancy in the U.S. twice that of England and Canada!).

But none of this mattered, because their coffers over-floweth, and Hallelujah, it is a great day for the Lord!

There is a cure--------Tell our right-wing hypocrites, who Judge, rather than "Judge not".... to shove it....

GOD

ABOUT THE AUTHOR: I was employed in our Criminal Justice System for a cumulative 20 years as a probation officer, with 5 of those years as a chief probation officer. I authored the concept of "Shock Incarceration" which became law in Kansas in 1970, and then was adopted in numerous jurisdictions in the U.S. and also spread to Europe—it is currently identified in the U.S. as "Boot Camp" [as the means to "shock" the young offender—and a total distortion of my original intent—like many ideas, once released, they take on a life of their own]. I also instigated establishment of the first Court Psychiatric Clinic in the U.S., in conjunction with psychiatrists from the Menninger Foundation, as a chief probation officer. Finally, I was the Democrat candidate for Congress, District 21, TX, 2000. I would most define myself as a Social Ecologist-- [albeit my degree is in Psychology]. My web page is www.Inclusivism.org —which has been on the internet since 1996.

http://www.amazon.com/James-L.-Jim-Green/e/B001KHZIMM/ref=ntt_dp_epwbk_0

A BRIEF ADDENDUM: When the U.S. Supreme Court denied certiorari—where the violation of my constitutional rights were obvious, and criminal negligence on the part of the government defendants in the death of our son, equally obvious—[detailed in THE HARVARD BOYS CLUB, Amazon/Kindle]--I filed a Petition for Rehearing [which is automatic]—and included the following. The Clerk of the U.S. Supreme Court called me at my work in California, and asked that I withdraw the "cartoon" [a reprint from The NEW YORKER] from my Petition. I refused on the basis of the First Amendment, and it remains in the archives at the U.S. Supreme Court [Docket #: 79-1627], to this day. The wording [not that clear] is: "Excellent, excellent. A fine blend of truths, half-truths, and blatant falsehoods".

IN THE

Supreme Court of the United States

October Term, 1979

No. 79-1627

JAMES L. GREEN,

Petitioner,

vs.

"Excellent, excellent. A fine blend of truths, half-truths, and blatant falsehoods."

OTHER BOOKS BY THIS AUTHOR ON AMAZON/KINDLE/BN:

•THE HARVARD BOYS CLUB: Hitler's Assault On Our Freedoms From His Grave

•MY LETTERS TO PRESIDENT OBAMA: Confessions Of A Compulsive Letter Writer

•OUR GREED AND IGNORANCE: Poses A Far Greater Threat To America, Than Terrorism

•LETTERS ON STEROIDS: Confessions Of A Compulsive Letter-To-The-Editor Writer

•THE FIRST TIME I HAD SEX: And, The Religious Intolerance Attack On America

•WHY PRESIDENT OBAMA LOST THE 2012 ELECTION: A Wake-Up Call

•ECONOMIC INCLUSIVISM: Neo-Capitalism/An Anthology: Inclusive pro-market solutions to our social problems

•AMERICA IS ONE SICK MF: Why Greed-Driven America Went Off The Rails....

•EVERY GIVEN SUNDAY: A Scientific Formula To Predict NFL Games

And others....http://www.amazon.com/James-L.-Jim-Green/e/B001KHZIMM/ref=ntt_dp_epwbk_0